The Freedom of Information Act (FOIA): Background, Legislation, and Policy Issues

Wendy Ginsberg
Analyst in American National Government

January 23, 2014

Congressional Research Service

7-5700

www.crs.gov

R41933

Summary

The Freedom of Information Act (FOIA; 5 U.S.C. §552) allows any person—individual or corporate, citizen or not—to request and obtain, without explanation or justification, existing, identifiable, and unpublished agency records on any topic. Pursuant to FOIA, the public has presumptive access to agency records unless the material falls within any of FOIA's nine categories of exception. Disputes over the release of records requested pursuant to FOIA can be appealed administratively, resolved through mediation, or heard in court.

FOIA is a tool of inquiry and information gathering for various sectors—including the media, businesses, scholars, attorneys, consumers, and activists. Agency responses to FOIA requests may involve a few sheets of paper, several linear feet of records, or information in an electronic format. Assembling responses requires staff time to search for records and make duplicates, among other resource commitments. Agency information management professionals are responsible for efficiently and economically responding to, or denying, FOIA requests.

FOIA was enacted in 1966, after 11 years of legislative development in the House, and nearly six years of consideration in the Senate. The perception that agencies were not properly implementing FOIA has resulted in amendments in 1974, 1976, 1986, 1996, 2007, and 2010.

In FY2012, the Department of Justice (DOJ) annual summary of agencies' FOIA administrative statistics found the federal government received the highest volume of requests since at least FY1998: 651,254 FOIA requests. Requests increased by 7,089 compared to FY2011 (a 1.1% increase). This increase is notably smaller than increases in recent years (in FY2011 requests were up 46,750, an increase of 7.8% from FY2010; in FY2010 requests were up 39,590, an increase of 7.7% from FY2009). The Department of Homeland Security (DHS) received more FOIA requests than any other agency with 190,589 requests in FY2012 (29.3% of all FOIA requests). The increase in requests in recent years, variation in other departments and agencies notwithstanding, was largely prompted by an increase in requests to DHS (particularly within the U.S. Citizenship and Immigration Service and U.S. Customs and Border Patrol). Increases in DHS requests made up 97.5% of the increase in requests governmentwide in FY2011 and 68.2% in FY2010. It is not clear what prompted the increase in requests in DHS. In contrast, the Department of Defense (DOD) saw an 8,039 (10.9%) reduction in the number of FOIA requests it received in FY2012.

On March 15, 2013, Representative Darrell E. Issa, chairman of the House Committee on Oversight and Government Reform, introduced the FOIA Act (H.R. 1211). The bill, among other requirements, seeks to amend FOIA by requiring agencies to update FOIA regulations to reflect statutory and policy changes to its implementation. The bill would create a pilot program to examine the applicability of automated and online systems to the FOIA request and appeal processes. H.R. 1211 would also enact into law the Obama Administration's policy of implementing FOIA pursuant to a presumption of openness.

This report provides background on FOIA, discusses the categories of records FOIA exempts from public release, and analyzes statistics on FOIA administration. The report also provides background on several legal and policy issues related to FOIA, including the release of controversial records, the growth in use of certain FOIA exemptions, and the adoption of new technologies to improve FOIA administration. The report concludes with an examination of potential FOIA-related policy options for the 113th Congress.

Contents

Introduction 1

FOIA Background 2
    FOIA Exemptions 3
    Obama Administration Initiatives 5
        Department of Justice Guidance 5
        Soliciting Public Input 6
        The Open Government Directive 6
        The Remaining Backlog 8

FOIA Statistics for FY2012 9
    FOIA Request Volume 9
    FOIA Processing 10

Costs to Administer FOIA 11

Recent and Ongoing Developments Related to FOIA 13
    The FOIA Oversight and Implementation Act of 2013 13
    Use and Growth of Exemptions 14
    Oversight of the Office of Government Information Services 15
    A Citizen's Guide to Using the Freedom of Information Act 17
    Releasing Controversial Information 17
        Photographs That Could Potentially Endanger U.S. Citizens 17
        Photographs and Video of Osama bin Laden 17
    The Release of White House Visitor Logs 18
    Operations of *FOIAonline* 20

Some Policy Options for the 113th Congress 20
    Monitoring the Expansion of b(3) Exemptions 20
    Consideration of Agencies' FOIA Culture 22
        The Department of Justice's Chief FOIA Officer Reports 22
        Improving Customer Service 23
        Updating Agencies' FOIA Regulations 23
    Status of White House Visitor Logs 24
    Examining the Progress of *FOIAonline* 24
    An Alternative for FOIA Implementation: Centralizing FOIA Processing 25

Figures

Figure 1. FOIA Backlog in the Federal Government 8

Figure 2. FOIA Requests Received by the Federal Government 10

Figure 3. FOIA Requests Received and Processed, and the Remaining FOIA Backlog 11

Figure 4. Costs of FOIA-Related Activities for Federal Departments and Agencies 13

Contacts

Author Contact Information 26

Acknowledgments 26

Introduction[1]

The Freedom of Information Act (FOIA; 5 U.S.C. §552), often referred to as the embodiment of "the people's right to know" about the activities and operations of government, statutorily established a presumption of public access to information held by executive branch departments and agencies. Enacted in 1966 to replace the "Public Information" section of the Administrative Procedure Act (APA; 5 U.S.C. Subchapter II),[2] FOIA allows any person—individual or corporate, citizen or not—to request and obtain, without explanation or justification, existing, identifiable, and unpublished agency records on any topic.[3]

Each new presidential administration has instructed agencies to implement FOIA differently. For example, the Department of Justice (DOJ) under the direction of the George W. Bush Administration cautioned federal agencies to give "full and deliberate consideration of the institutional, commercial, and personal privacy interests when making disclosure determinations" and assured them that DOJ would defend agency decisions in court "unless they lack[ed] a sound legal basis or present[ed] an unwarranted risk of adverse impact on the ability of other agencies to protect other important records."[4] In contrast, the Barack H. Obama Administration requires agencies "to adopt a presumption in favor of disclosure."[5]

The 113th Congress may have an interest in the implementation of FOIA and whether that implementation appropriately reflects the law. In addition to agency oversight, Congress may have particular interest in exploring some of the following FOIA-related issues:

- whether to limit, maintain, or expand the number of statutes that permit agencies to withhold certain information from public release;
- whether to require departments and agencies to update their FOIA regulations to reflect statutory changes to the law;
- how to assist agencies in reducing FOIA request backlogs;
- whether White House visitor logs, portions of which are currently made public pursuant to Obama Administration policy, include appropriate and necessary information;
- whether the Environmental Protection Agency's new *FOIA Online* tool streamlines the administration of FOIA requests and reduces implementation costs; and

---

[1] Parts of this report are adapted from CRS Report RL32780, *Freedom of Information Act (FOIA) Amendments: 110th Congress*, by Harold C. Relyea.

[2] The "Public Information" section was formerly Sec. 3 of the Administrative Procedure Act. (P.L. 79-404; 60 Stat. 238).

[3] The Intelligence Authorization for Fiscal Year 2003 amended FOIA to preclude agencies of the intelligence community from disclosing records in response to FOIA requests made by any foreign government or international government organization. Intelligence Authorization Act for Fiscal Year 2003, (P.L. 107-306, §312, codified at 5 U.S.C. §552(a)(3)(E)).

[4] Memorandum from Attorney General John Ashcroft for *Heads of Federal Departments and Agencies: Freedom of Information Act*, October 12, 2001, at http://www.justice.gov/archive/oip/011012 htm.

[5] Memorandum from President Barack Obama for *Heads of Executive Departments and Agencies: Freedom of Information Act*, January 21, 2009, at http://www.whitehouse.gov/the_press_office/FreedomofInformationAct/.

- whether to shift FOIA implementation by centralizing it in a single entity, rather than continue its implementation within each individual agency.

This report discusses FOIA's history, examines its implementation, and discusses policy options for the 113th Congress.

FOIA Background[6]

FOIA's history is an essential component of understanding the act's scope and its utility. FOIA applies only to the departments and agencies of the federal executive branch, and serves as the foundation for public oversight and transparency of executive branch operations.[7] FOIA is the primary tool for the public to access federal executive branch records.

The scope of FOIA has been shaped by both historical and constitutional factors. During the latter half of the 1950s, when congressional subcommittees examined government information availability, the practices of federal departments and agencies were a primary focus. The public, the press, and even some congressional committees and subcommittees were sometimes rebuffed when seeking information from executive branch entities.[8] At the time, the preservation of, and access to, presidential records had not yet become a great public or congressional concern, so the records were ultimately not covered by FOIA.[9]

The accessibility of federal court records and congressional records, likewise, was not a primary congressional concern. Some Members and academics have asserted that, in the case of Congress, the secret journal clause or the speech or debate clause of the Constitution[10] could be

---

[6] For a more in-depth legislative history of FOIA, see CRS Report RL32780, *Freedom of Information Act (FOIA) Amendments: 110th Congress*, by Harold C. Relyea.

[7] At present, FOIA makes the requirements of the statute applicable only to an "agency," which "means each authority of the Government of the United States, whether or not it is within or subject to review by another agency, but does not include - (A) the Congress; or (B) the courts of the United States[.]" (5 U.S.C. §551)

The committees that developed FOIA—the House Committee on Government Operations (now known as the House Oversight and Government Reform Committee) and the Senate Committee on the Judiciary—were responding to perceived secrecy problems in the executive branch. Thus, FOIA was created, approved, and implemented with an executive branch focus. For more information on the limitations of FOIA applicability see Harold C. Relyea, "Congress and Freedom of Information: A Retrospective and a Look at the Current Issue," *Government Information Quarterly*, vol. 26 (2009), pp. 437-440.

[8] Sen. Edward Kennedy, "The Freedom of Information Act Experience," remarks in the Senate, *Congressional Record*, September 22, 1976, p. 31823. Senator Kennedy submitted for printing into the *Record* a document written by Harold C. Relyea entitled "The Provision of Government Information: The Federal Freedom of Information Act Experience." This reference cites to Mr. Relyea's document.

[9] For more information on preservation of and access to presidential records and vice presidential records, see CRS Report R40238, *The Presidential Records Act: Background and Recent Issues for Congress*, by Wendy Ginsberg.

[10] U.S. Constitution, Article I, Section 5, clause 3, which directs each house of Congress to keep a journal of its proceedings and publish the same, except such parts as may be judged to require secrecy, has been interpreted to authorize the House and the Senate to keep certain records secret. See, for example, the National Constitution Center, "Interactive Constitution," at http://ratify.constitutioncenter.org/constitution/details_explanation.php?link=010&const=01_art_01. U.S. Constitution, Article 1, Section 6, clause 1, which specifies that Members of Congress, "for any Speech or Debate in either House ... shall not be questioned in any other Place," might be regarded as a bar to requests to Members for records concerning their floor, committee, subcommittee, or legislative activity. For more information on the Speech or Debate clause, see CRS Legal Sidebar WSLG190, Speech or Debate Clause Immunity for Members and Staff, by Alissa M. Dolan.

impediments to the effective application of FOIA to Congress.[11] In a 1955 hearing, Representative John E. Moss, chairman of the newly created Special Subcommittee on Government Information, delineated the intended scope of freedom of information legislation, saying,

> We are not studying the availability of information from Congress, although many comments have been made by the press in that field, but we are taking a long, hard look at the amount of information available from the executive and independent agencies for both the public and its elected representatives.[12]

Eleven years after that hearing, FOIA was enacted and was made applicable only to federal, executive-branch departments and agencies. At the time of its enactment, FOIA was regarded as a somewhat revolutionary law. Only two other nations—Sweden and Finland—had comparable disclosure laws, and neither statute was as sweeping as the new American model. The law's premise reversed the burden of proof that had existed under the public information section of the APA, which required requesters to establish a justification or a need for the information being sought.[13] Under FOIA, in contrast, access is presumed—although presidential Administrations have interpreted this presumed access differently. Agencies must justify denying access to requested information.

FOIA's enactment was unusual in another regard: no executive branch department or agency head had supported the legislation, and President Lyndon B. Johnson was reportedly reluctant to sign the measure.[14] The law was not, and may continue not to be enthusiastically received by the executive branch. Supporters of FOIA, therefore, have maintained that its implementation and use may require close attention from congressional overseers.[15]

FOIA Exemptions

FOIA exempts nine categories of records from the statute's rule of disclosure.[16] The exemptions are as follows:

---

[11] See U.S. Congress, Senate Committee on Governmental Affairs, *To Eliminate Congressional and Federal Double Standards*, hearing, 96th Cong., 1st sess., September 20, 1979 (Washington: GPO, 1979); Harold C. Relyea, "Public Access to Congressional Records: Present Policy and Reform Considerations," *Government Information Quarterly*, vol. 2, 1985, pp. 235-256.

[12] U.S. Congress, House Committee on Government Operations, *Availability of Information from Federal Departments and Agencies*, hearing, 84th Cong., 1st sess., November 7, 1955 (Washington: GPO, 1956), p. 3.

[13] Sen. Edward Kennedy, "The Freedom of Information Act Experience," remarks in the Senate, *Congressional Record*, September 22, 1976, vol. 122, part 25, p. 31822. Senator Kennedy submitted for printing into the *Record* a document written by Harold C. Relyea entitled "The Provision of Government Information: The Federal Freedom of Information Act Experience." This reference cites Mr. Relyea's document.

[14] See Samuel J. Archibald, "The Freedom of Information Act Revisited," *Public Administration Review*, vol. 39, July-August 1979, pp. 311-318. See also "NOW With Bill Moyers – Politics and Economy: Bill Moyers on the Freedom of Information Act," April, 5, 2002, at http://www.pbs.org/now/commentary/moyers4.html. According to Moyers, Johnson "had to be dragged kicking and screaming to the signing ceremony. He hated the very idea of the Freedom of Information Act; hated the thought of journalists rummaging in government closets; hated them challenging the official view of reality." See also Harold C. Relyea, "Federal Freedom of Information Policy: Highlights of Recent Developments," *Government Information Quarterly*, vol. 26 (January 2009), p. 314.

[15] For a detailed history of amendments to FOIA, see out-of-print CRS Report R40766, *Freedom of Information Act (FOIA): Issues for the 111th Congress*, by Wendy Ginsberg, available from the author upon request.

[16] 5 U.S.C. §552(b).

1. Information properly classified for national defense or foreign policy purposes as secret under criteria established by an executive order;
2. Information relating solely to agency internal personnel rules and practices;
3. Data specifically exempted from disclosure by a statute other than FOIA if that statute
    a. requires that the data be withheld from the public in such a manner as to leave no discretion on the issue;
    b. establishes particular criteria for withholding information or refers to particular types of matters to be withheld; or
    c. specifically cites to this exemption (if the statute is enacted after October 28, 2009, the date of enactment of the OPEN FOIA Act of 2009;[17]
4. Trade secrets and commercial or financial information obtained from a person that is privileged or confidential;
5. Inter- or intra-agency memoranda or letters that would not be available by law except to an agency in litigation;
6. Personnel, medical, or similar files, the disclosure of which would constitute an unwarranted invasion of personal privacy;
7. Certain kinds of records compiled for law enforcement purposes;
8. Certain information relating to the regulation of financial institutions; and
9. Geological and geophysical information and data.

Some of these exemptions, such as the one concerning trade secrets and commercial or financial information, have been litigated and undergone considerable judicial interpretation.[18]

A person denied access to requested records, in whole or in part, may make an administrative appeal to the head of the agency for reconsideration. If an agency appeal is denied, an appeal for further consideration may be made in federal district court.[19] The Office of Government Information Services (OGIS), which was created within the National Archives and Records Administration (NARA), also may provide "mediation services to resolve disputes between persons making requests under this section and administrative agencies as a non-exclusive alternative to litigation."[20] OGIS services are advisory and nonbinding. The creation and role of OGIS will be discussed in more detail later in this report.

---

[17] P.L. 111-83); 123 Stat. 2142.

[18] For sources concerning judicial interpretation of FOIA, see Harry A. Hammitt, Marc Rotenberg, John A. Verdi and Mark S. Zaid, eds., *Litigation Under the Federal Open Government Laws: 2010*, fifth edition (Washington: EPIC Publications and The James Madison Project, 2008); James T. O'Reilly, *Federal Information Disclosure*, third edition (Eagan, MN: West Group, first published in 2000, with supplements); and U.S. Department of Justice, *Freedom of Information Act Guide*, June 2009 edition (Washington, DC: GPO, 2009), at http://www.justice.gov/oip/foia_guide09.htm.

[19] 5 U.S.C. §552(4)(B). See U.S. Congress, House Committee on Government Reform, *A Citizen's Guide on Using the Freedom of Information Act and the Privacy Act of 1974 to Request Government Records*, H.Rept. 109-226, 109th Cong., 1st sess. (Washington: GPO, 2005).

[20] 5 U.S.C. §552(h)(3).

Obama Administration Initiatives

On January 21, 2009, President Obama issued a memorandum on FOIA, stating that the act "should be administered with a clear presumption: In the face of doubt, openness prevails."[21] The memorandum stated that under the new administration

> All agencies should adopt a presumption in favor of disclosure, in order to renew their commitment to the principles embodied in FOIA, and to usher in a new era of open Government. The presumption of disclosure should be applied to all decisions involving FOIA.[22]

The memorandum directed the Attorney General to "issue new guidelines governing the FOIA to the heads of executive departments and agencies, reaffirming the commitment to accountability and transparency, and to publish such guidelines in the *Federal Register*."[23]

Department of Justice Guidance

On March 19, 2009, Attorney General Eric Holder issued a memorandum in which he required "A Presumption of Openness." The memorandum explicitly rescinded former Attorney General John Ashcroft's October 12, 2001, memorandum. Holder's memorandum read as follows:

> First, an agency should not withhold information simply because it may do so legally.... An agency should not withhold records merely because it can demonstrate, as a technical matter, that the records fall within the scope of a FOIA exemption.
>
> Second, whenever an agency determines that it cannot make full disclosure of a requested record, it must consider whether it can make partial disclosure. Agencies should always be mindful that the FOIA requires them to take reasonable steps to segregate and release nonexempt information. Even if some parts of a record must be withheld, other parts either may not be covered by a statutory exemption, or may be covered only in a technical sense unrelated to the actual impact of disclosure.
>
> At the same time, the disclosure obligation under the FOIA is not absolute....
>
> [T]he Department of Justice will defend a denial of a FOIA request only if (1) the agency reasonably foresees that disclosure would harm an interest protected by one of the statutory exemptions, or (2) disclosure is prohibited by law.[24]

The Obama and Holder memoranda reflected a shift from the memoranda of the George W. Bush Administration, which required agency and department heads to release documents "only after

---

[21] Memorandum from President Barack Obama for *Heads of Executive Departments and Agencies: Freedom of Information Act*, January 21, 2009, at http://www.whitehouse.gov/the_press_office/FreedomofInformationAct/.

[22] Ibid.

[23] Ibid.

[24] U.S. Department of Justice, Attorney General Eric Holder, *Memorandum For the Heads of Executive Departments and Agencies: The Freedom of Information Act (FOIA)*, Washington, DC, March 19, 2009, pp. 1-2, at http://www.usdoj.gov/ag/foia-memo-march2009.pdf.

full and deliberate consideration of the institutional, commercial, and personal privacy interests that could be implicated by disclosure of the information."[25]

Within the Department of Justice, the Office of Information Policy (OIP) is charged with "encouraging agency compliance" with FOIA and "ensuring that the President's FOIA memorandum and the Attorney General's FOIA Guidelines are fully implemented across the government."[26] To perform these duties, OIP "develops and issues policy guidance" on FOIA implementation and maintains and makes publicly available the *United States Department of Justice Guide to the Freedom of Information Act*, which provides history and case law related to FOIA.[27]

Soliciting Public Input

In 2009, the Obama Administration solicited information and ideas from the public on ways to make FOIA a more useful tool. From May 21 to July 6, for example, the Administration held a three-phase "Open Government Initiative" aimed at collecting ideas from the public on how to make government more collaborative, transparent, and participatory. The Administration sought public comment on "innovative approaches to policy, specific project suggestions, government-wide or agency-specific instructions, and any relevant examples and stories relating to law, policy, technology, culture, or practice."[28]

The Open Government Directive

On December 8, 2009, President Obama released his Open Government Directive—a presidential memorandum describing how agencies were to implement the open government and transparency values he discussed in earlier Administration memoranda.[29] The directive restated the Administration's commitment to the "principle that openness is the Federal Government's default position for FOIA issues."[30] The directive also encouraged agencies to release data and information "online in an open format that can be retrieved, downloaded, indexed, and searched by commonly used applications."[31] The information, according to the directive, was to be placed online even prior to a FOIA request, to preempt the need for such requests.[32] Pursuant to the

---

[25] John Ashcroft, U.S. Attorney General, *Memorandum for the Heads of all Federal Departments and Agencies: The Freedom of Information Act*, October 12, 2001, at http://www.doi.gov/foia/foia.pdf.

[26] U.S. Department of Justice, "About Us," at http://www.justice.gov/oip/about-us.html.

[27] Ibid. The *United States Department of Justice Guide to the Freedom of Information Act* is available at http://www.justice.gov/oip/foia_guide09 htm.

[28] National Academy of Public Administration (NAPA), *Open Government Dialogue*, May 21, 2009, at http://opengov.ideascale.com/akira/panel.do?id=4049. When the dialogue began, users could offer ideas without signing up for a log-on identity. On May 23, 2009, NAPA changed that policy and required all participants to log into the website before their comments could be posted.

[29] Executive Office of the President, Office of Management and Budget, *Memorandum for the Heads of Executive Departments and Agencies: Open Government Directive*, Washington, DC, December 8, 2009, at http://www.whitehouse.gov/omb/assets/memoranda_2010/m10-06.pdf. For a history and analysis of the Open Government Directive, see CRS Report R42817, *Government Transparency and Secrecy: An Examination of Meaning and Its Use in the Executive Branch*, by Wendy Ginsberg et al.

[30] Executive Office of the President, Office of Management and Budget, *Memorandum for the Heads of Executive Departments and Agencies: Open Government Directive*, p. 1.

[31] Ibid.

[32] Publishing agency records online is one suggestion that was repeated by several members of the public who (continued...)

memorandum, agencies were required to put their annual FOIA report on the Open Government website in an accessible format.

The Obama Administration directive required agencies with a backlog of FOIA requests to reduce the number of outstanding requests by 10% per year,[33] but did not state how the Administration would address agencies that do not comply with its requirements. Moreover, a reduction in backlog does not necessarily mean an agency is more efficiently administering FOIA. For example, an agency could eliminate a backlog by denying complex requests that could otherwise be released in part. Denying requests may take less time than negotiating a partial release. Additionally, some agencies may have reduced their backlog simply because they received fewer requests and not because they applied FOIA more effectively.

On March 16, 2010, then-White House Chief of Staff Rahm Emanuel and then-Counsel to the President Bob Bauer released an additional memorandum stating their appreciation for current agency efforts to implement the FOIA in accordance with the Administration's directives, but also said "more work remains to be done."[34] The memorandum instructed department and agency heads to "update all FOIA guidance and training materials to include the principles articulated in the President's [January 21, 2009] Memorandum."[35] It then asked department and agency heads to "assess whether [they] are devoting adequate resources to responding to FOIA requests promptly and cooperatively, consistent with the requirements for addressing this Presidential priority."[36]

Advocates of access to government records and information have stated the Obama Administration's efforts to make government more transparent and to make federal records more accessible have seen mixed results. In December 2012, the Transactional Records Access Clearinghouse (TRAC), a research center at Syracuse University that collects FOIA data from federal agencies, found that more FOIA-related lawsuits were filed during the first term of President Obama (720 FOIA-related lawsuits) than were filed in the second term of President George W. Bush (562 FOIA-related lawsuits).[37] OpenTheGovernment.org, a coalition that aims to make the "federal government a more open place,"[38] said the Administration's "[e]fforts to open the government continue to be frustrated by a governmental predisposition towards secrecy, especially in the national security bureaucracy."[39] In a February 2013 open letter to the President that addressed transparency, generally, OpenTheGovernment.org wrote:

(...continued)
participated in the Open Government Initiative's online collaboration.

[33] According to FOIA.gov, a backlogged request is "pending beyond the statutory time period for a response." A backlogged request is different from a pending request, which is a "FOIA request or administrative appeal for which an agency has not yet taken final action in all respects." See U.S. Department of Justice, "FOIA.gov: Glossary," at http://www.foia.gov/glossary.html#.

[34] The White House, Rahm Emanuel and Bob Bauer, *Memorandum for Agency and Department Heads: Freedom of Information Act*, March 16, 2010, at http://www.whitehouse.gov/sites/default/files/rss_viewer/foia_memo_3-16-10.pdf.

[35] Ibid.

[36] Ibid.

[37] The FOIA Project, "FOIA Lawsuits Increase During Obama Administration," December 20, 2012, at http://foiaproject.org/2012/12/20/increase-in-foia-lawsuits-during-obama-administration/.

[38] OpenTheGovernment.org, "We Are," at http://www.openthegovernment.org/we_are.

[39] "2012 Secrecy Report—Sunlight Overshadowed," *Openthegovernment.org*, September 12, 2012, press release, at http://www.openthegovernment.org/node/3578.

> We applaud the strides made during your first term to proactively release more information online, including on such sites as *data.gov*, *recovery.gov* and *USAspending.gov*. But more can be done toward achieving transparency.[40]

The Remaining Backlog

According to *FOIA.gov*, an online portal that includes agency-reported FOIA administration statistics, executive branch agencies have significantly reduced their backlogged requests when compared to data collected prior to 2009, although the largest reductions occurred before President Obama issued the December 2009 Open Government Directive. The number of backlogged requests at executive branch agencies dropped from 130,419 at the end of FY2008 to 75,594 at the end of FY2009 (a 42% reduction), and to 69,526 at the end of FY2010 (another 8% decline).[41] In that time, the Department of Homeland Security (DHS) alone reduced its backlog from 74,879 at the end of FY2008 to 18,918 at the end of FY2009 (a 74.7% reduction), and to 11,383 at the end of FY2010 (another 39.8% decline).[42] Therefore, variations in other departments and agencies notwithstanding, DHS alone accounted for a majority of the government-wide reductions in FOIA backlogs during this period.

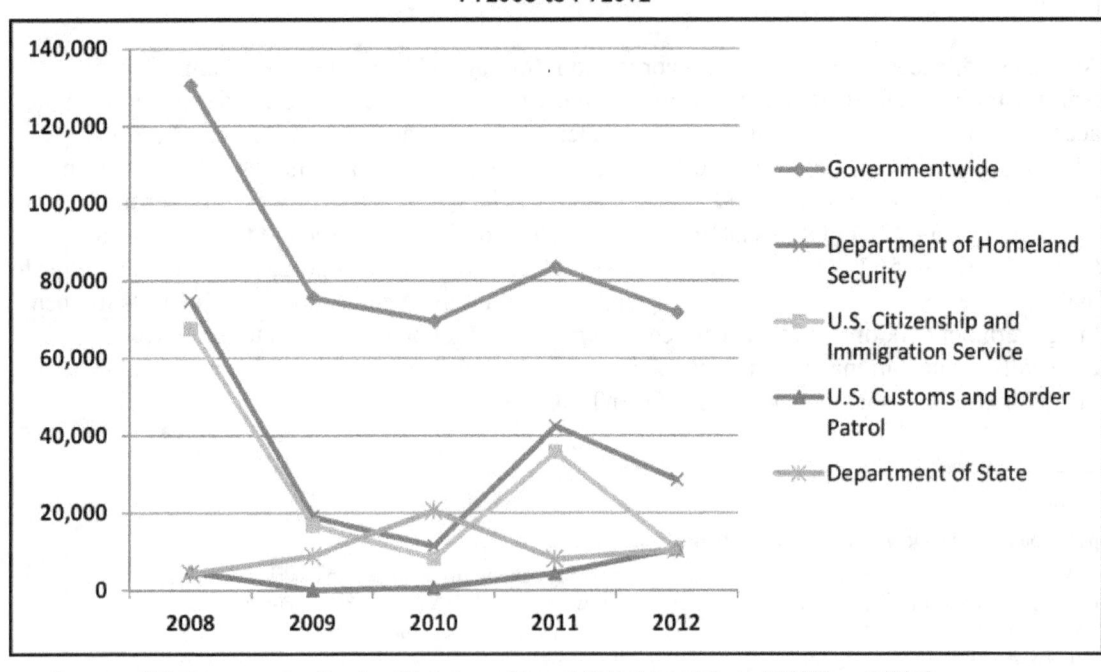

Figure 1. FOIA Backlog in the Federal Government
FY2008 to FY2012

Source: U.S. Department of Justice, "*Summary of Annual FOIA Reports*" from FY2008 to FY2012, at http://www.justice.gov/oip/reports.html. Data are also available at Data.gov.

Notes: The Department of Homeland Security (DHS) was the federal entity that reported the largest number of backlogged requests in FY2012. The U.S. Citizenship and Immigration Services and the U.S. Customs and Border

---

[40] OpenTheGovernment.org, "Dear Mr. President: Here's How to Secure Your Open Government Legacy," at http://www.openthegovernment.org/node/3858.

[41] Data are available at U.S. Department of Justice, "FOIA.gov," at http://www.foia.gov/index.html.

[42] Ibid.

Patrol were the two agencies within DHS that reported the largest backlogs. According to CRS's analysis of DOJ's summary report, in FY2012, DHS reported 39.8% of all FOIA backlogged requests government-wide.

From FY2008 to FY2011, the federal government overall, as well as particular departments and agencies, did not meet the Open Government Directive's requirement to reduce FOIA backlogs by 10% each year. According to DOJ's FY2011 summary, the FOIA government-wide backlog increased by 13,964 requests from FY2010 to FY2011 (agencies reported 83,490 backlogged requests in FY2011, a 20.1% increase from FY2010).[43] Although many agencies increased their backlog from FY2010 to FY2011, the Department of State decreased its backlog by 12,440 requests (from 20, 518 requests to 8,078 requests from FY2010 to FY2011). In FY2012, however, this trend ceased. Instead, the federal government overall was able to decrease its backlog of pending FOIA requests in FY2012 by 14.0%.[44] DHS, which accounted for more than half of the government's total backlog in FY2011,[45] reduced its backlog in FY2012 by 32.7%.

FOIA Statistics for FY2012

FOIA Request Volume

The Department of Justice (DOJ) found that in FY2012 the federal government received the highest volume of FOIA requests since at least FY1998: 651,254 FOIA requests.[46] Requests increased by 7,089 when compared to FY2011 (a 1.1% increase). This increase is notably smaller than increases in recent years (in FY2011 requests were up 46,750, an increase of 7.8%; in FY2010 requests were up 39,590, an increase of 7.71%) and may have contributed to the federal government's ability to decrease backlogged FOIA requests.

In FY2012, DHS received more requests than any other agency with 190,589 requests (29.3% of all FOIA requests).[47] DHS requests increased by 14,933 from FY2011 to FY2012, which is also a smaller increase in requests than DHS has received in recent years.[48] From FY2009 to FY2010

---

[43] Ibid.

[44] Department of Justice, "Summary of Annual FOIA Reports for FY2012," p.7, at http://www.justice.gov/oip/docs/fy-2012-annual-report-summary.pdf.

[45] Department of Justice, "Summary of Annual FOIA Reports for FY2011," p.10, at http://www.justice.gov/oip/docs/fy-2011-annual-report-summary.pdf

[46] Department of Justice, "Summary of Annual FOIA Reports for FY2012," p.2 at http://www.justice.gov/oip/docs/fy-2012-annual-report-summary.pdf.

[47] The Department of Homeland Security's (DHS's) FOIA logs do not provide details on what types of requests or policy changes could be prompting the increase in FOIA requests. DHS, however, has, since 2007, adopted a policy that allows non-U.S. citizens and nonresident aliens to use FOIA to request immigration-related information. See Hugo Teufel III, *Privacy Policy Guidance Memorandum*, U.S. Department of Homeland Security, Memorandum Number 2007-1, Washington, DC, January 19, 2007, at http://www.dhs.gov/xlibrary/assets/privacy/privacy_policyguide_2007-1.pdf. Pursuant to the Privacy Act (5 U.S.C. §552a), U.S. citizens and permanent resident aliens have presumptive access to personally identifiable files on themselves held by federal agencies—generally excepting law enforcement and intelligence entities. Noncitizens and nonresident aliens, however, can request personally identifiable records from DHS pursuant to Memorandum Number 2007-1. According to the policy, "[n]on-U.S. persons have the right of access to their [personally identifiable information] and the right to amend their records, absent an exemption under the Privacy Act; however, this policy does not extend or create a right of judicial review for non-U.S. persons" (p. 2). In many cases, it appears these non-U.S. citizen requests are recorded as FOIA requests. Increasing use of FOIA to access noncitizens' personally identifiable records may be a cause of DHS's increasing requests.

[48] Data are available at U.S. Department of Justice, "FOIA.gov," at http://www.foia.gov/index.html.

DHS requests were up by 27,005 requests; from FY2010 to FY2011, DHS requests were up by 45,558 requests. U.S. Citizenship and Immigration Service and U.S. Customs and Border Patrol within DHS saw the majority of the increases in requests in these years. It is not clear whether any new policy or regulation prompted the increase in requests. DHS's Chief FOIA Officer, in the agency's annual 2011 FOIA report, wrote that the increase in requests demonstrated "acceptance among the public" of "government accountability through the Freedom of Information Act."[49] Other possible contributors to the increase in FOIA requests include, changes in immigration law or policy; use of less efficient methods to receive and respond to FOIA requests (for example, a continued reliance on paper rather than an electronic database to receive requests or find and provide records); and encouragement of stakeholder organizations to have members file FOIA requests.

Figure 2. FOIA Requests Received by the Federal Government
FY2008 to FY2012

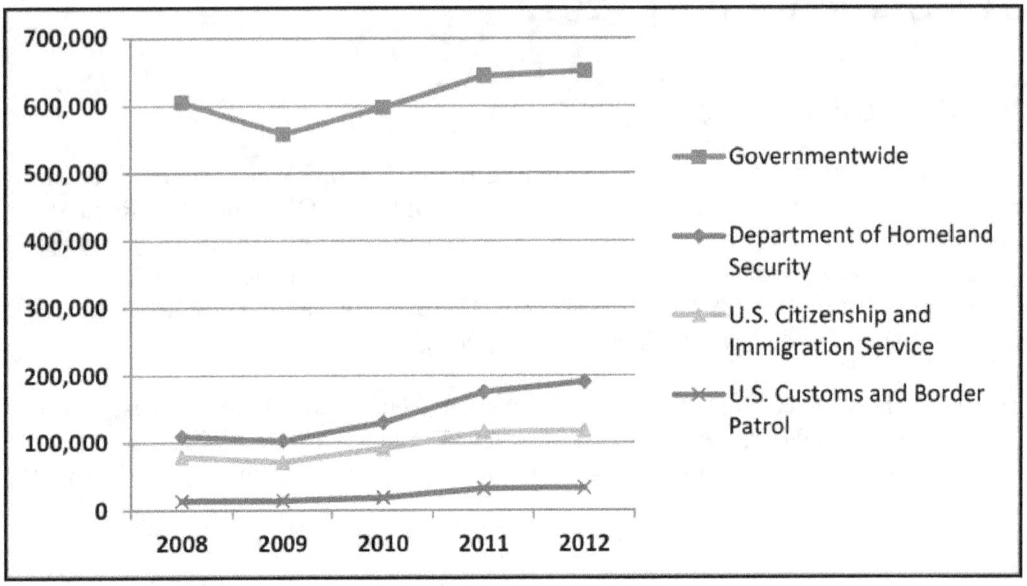

Source: U.S. Department of Justice, "Summary of Annual FOIA Reports" from FY2008 to FY2012, at http://www.justice.gov/oip/reports.html.

Notes: The Department of Homeland Security (DHS) was the federal entity that received the largest number of requests in FY2012. The U.S. Citizenship and Immigration Services and the U.S. Customs and Border Patrol were the two agencies within DHS that received the largest number of requests. According to DOJ's summary report, in FY2012, DHS reported it received 29.3% of all FOIA requests received government-wide.

FOIA Processing

Figure 3, below, shows that executive branch agencies processed more FOIA requests in FY2012 than it processed in any of the previous four fiscal years. In fact, the increase in FOIA requests processed by the agencies outpaced the increase in requests received. This most likely contributed to the federal government's ability to decrease backlogged FOIA requests by 14.0%.

---

[49] U.S. Department of Homeland Security, "2011 Freedom of Information Act Report to the Attorney General of the United States," February 2012, p. ii, at http://www.dhs.gov/xlibrary/assets/privacy/privacy-foia-annual-report-fy-2011-dhs.pdf.

For instance, in FY2012, DOJ's summary report showed that departments and agencies processed 665,924 requests, which was 34,500 more requests than in FY2011 (5.5% more).[50] The federal government, in fact, processed 14,670 more requests in FY2012 than it received. In FY2012, DHS processed more FOIA requests than any other department or agency, with 205,895 requests—which is 60,264 more requests than the 145,631 FOIA requests DHS processed in FY2011.[51] In FY2012, DHS processed 15,306 more requests than it received (190,589). In FY2012—as it did in all other years analyzed, DHS received more FOIA requests than any other federal agency.

Figure 3. FOIA Requests Received and Processed, and the Remaining FOIA Backlog
FY2008 to FY2012

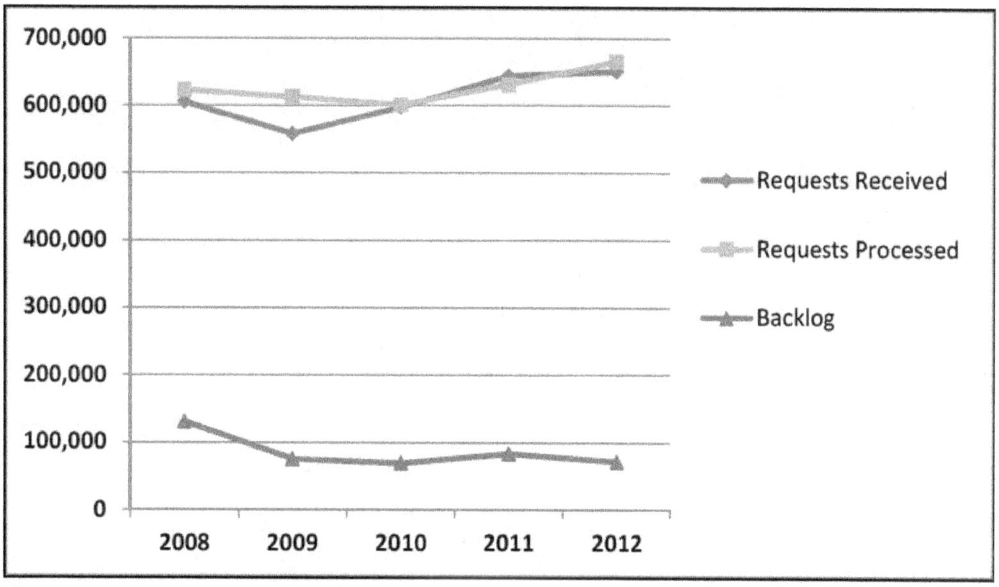

Source: U.S. Department of Justice, "Summary of Annual FOIA Reports" from FY2008 to FY2012, at http://www.justice.gov/oip/reports.html.

Costs to Administer FOIA

As shown in **Figure 4**, costs to administer FOIA rose from FY2008 to FY2011 and then decreased from FY2011 to FY2012.[52] In FY2012, the latest full year for which cost information is available, the total cost of all FOIA-related activities for all federal departments and agencies, as reported in their annual FOIA reports, was an estimated $429.6 million.[53] The data reflect a

---

[50] Department of Justice, "Summary of Annual FOIA Reports for FY2012," p.3 at http://www.justice.gov/oip/docs/fy-2012-annual-report-summary.pdf.

[51] U.S. Department of Justice, "Summary of Annual FOIA Reports for FY2012," p.3 at http://www.justice.gov/oip/docs/fy-2012-annual-report-summary.pdf;

U.S. Department of Justice, "Summary of Annual FOIA Reports for FY2011," p.3 at http://www.justice.gov/oip/foiapost/fy-2011-annual-report-summary.pdf.

[52] U.S. Department of Justice, Summary of Annual FOIA Reports, FY2006 through FY2012. All reports are available on DOJ's website at http://www.justice.gov/oip/reports.html.

[53] U.S. Department of Justice, "Summary of Annual FOIA Reports for FY2012," p.17 at http://www.justice.gov/oip/docs/fy-2012-annual-report-summary.pdf. FOIA.gov does not include data on FOIA processing costs.

decrease of $6.2 million in administrative costs from FY2011.[54] According to DOJ's summary of FOIA reports, in FY2012, $24.2 million (5.6%) of the federal government's reported FOIA costs were spent on "litigation activities."[55] In FY2011, litigation-related costs were 5.4% ($23.4 million) of all FOIA costs.[56]

One possible driver of the decrease in FOIA costs is the reduction of "full-time FOIA staff" dedicated to administering the act.[57] FY2012 is the first year since FY2008 that the federal government has decreased the number of full-time FOIA staff (in FY2011 full-time FOIA staff were 4,369; in FY2012 full-time FOIA staff were 4,065).[58] Most of the reduction of full-time FOIA staff occurred within DOD.[59]

---

[54] U.S. Department of Justice, "Summary of Annual FOIA Reports for FY2011," p.21 at http://www.justice.gov/oip/docs/ fy-2011-annual-report-summary.pdf.

[55] U.S. Department of Justice, "Summary of Annual FOIA Reports for FY2012," p.17 at http://www.justice.gov/oip/docs/ fy-2012-annual-report-summary.pdf.

[56] U.S. Department of Justice, "Summary of Annual FOIA Reports for FY2011," p.22 at http://www.justice.gov/oip/docs/ fy-2011-annual-report-summary.pdf.

[57] Pursuant to DOJ guidance, "full-time FOIA staff" is calculated by adding together the number of "equivalent full-time FOIA employees" and "full-time FOIA staff." These counting guidelines were first applied in agencies' FY2008 annual FOIA reports. DOJ, in its "Summary of Annual FOIA Reports for FY2008," wrote that the change in guidelines for counting staffing levels would make it "possible to compare these staffing numbers from year to year." See U.S. Department of Justice, "Summary of Annual FOIA Reports for Fiscal Year 2008," at http://www.justice.gov/oip/foiapost/2009foiapost16 htm.

[58] U.S. Department of Justice, "Summary of Annual FOIA Reports for FY2012," p.16 at http://www.justice.gov/oip/docs/fy-2012-annual-report-summary.pdf.

[59] DOD's FY2012 Annual FOIA Report does not address why the department has reduced its full-time FOIA staff. (U.S. Department of Defense, "FY2012 Annual FOIA Report, at http://www.dod mil/pubs/foi/dfoipo/docs/DoDFY2012AnnualFOIA_Report.pdf.)

Figure 4. Costs of FOIA-Related Activities for Federal Departments and Agencies
FY2006 to FY2012

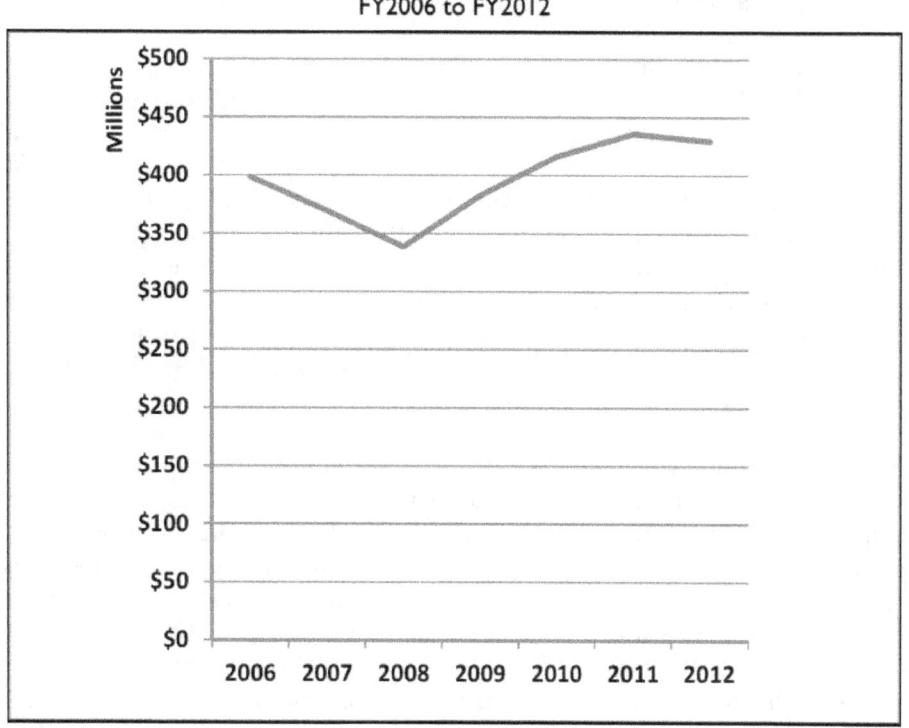

Source: Department of Justice "Summary of Annual FOIA Reports" from FY2006 through FY2012. All summary reports are available at http://www.justice.gov/oip/reports.html.

Recent and Ongoing Developments Related to FOIA

In recent years, Congress has considered a range of FOIA-related matters, including The FOIA Oversight and Implementation Act of 2013 (H.R. 1211). Additionally, the 113th Congress may have an interest in creating new or limiting the use of FOIA exemptions or determining whether the executive branch should be releasing certain controversial records—including photographs related to the death of Osama Bin Laden or visitor logs at the White House.

The FOIA Oversight and Implementation Act of 2013

On March 15, 2013, Representatives Darrell E. Issa and Elijah E. Cummings, the chairman and ranking member, respectively, of the Committee on Government Oversight and Reform, introduced the FOIA Oversight and Implementation Act of 2013 (FOIA Act; H.R. 1211). The legislation seeks to amend FOIA and its implementation in a number of ways. For instance, the legislation would enact into law the Obama Administration's policy that FOIA should be administered with a presumption of openness. This policy was outlined by Attorney General Eric Holder in a 2009 memorandum in which he stated that agencies should only withhold information in instances of foreseeable harm.[60] The bill would also amend FOIA by requiring that agencies

---

[60] U.S. Department of Justice, Attorney General Eric Holder, *Memorandum For the Heads of Executive Departments and Agencies: The Freedom of Information Act (FOIA)*, Washington, DC, March 19, 2009, pp. 1-2, at (continued...)

"make available for public inspection" records requested three or more times. The bill would also require agencies to proactively release records of public interest online.[61]

In addition, the bill would require the creation of a pilot program to examine the applicability of automated and online FOIA request intake and responses through the *FOIAonline* system. *FOIAonline* is an online portal that allows the public to submit FOIA requests electronically and track the progress of their requests. The *FOIAonline* portal also allows agencies to provide responsive records to the requester (and concurrently to the general public) using the portal, among other operations.[62] Six federal agencies currently participate in *FOIAonline*.[63] The bill would statutorily require the Director of the Office of Management and Budget to select three agencies, of varying sizes and that have not previously participated in *FOIAonline*, to employ the *FOIAonline* system. The FOIA Act would require all agencies to participate in an automated FOIA administration website such as *FOIAonline*.[64] *FOIAonline* is discussed in further detail in the section *Operations of FOIAonline* in this report.

H.R. 1211 also seeks to strengthen the Office of Government Information Services (OGIS), which is sometimes referred to as the "the FOIA ombudsman," by granting it greater independence and expanding its responsibilities and reporting requirements.[65] Furthermore, to ensure that agencies implement the FOIA Oversight and Implementation Act of 2013, the legislation mandates that agencies update their FOIA regulations within 180 days of the bill's enactment. This requirement in the legislation may be a response to some agencies' failure to update their FOIA regulations to reflect the Attorney General's 2009 memorandum or the OPEN Government Act of 2007. Agency compliance with FOIA policy is discussed further in the *Consideration of FOIA Culture* section of this report.

On July 16, 2013, H.R. 1211 was reported by the Committee on Oversight and Government Reform and placed on the calendar. No companion legislation currently exists in the Senate.

Use and Growth of Exemptions

Pursuant to FOIA's third exemption, 5 U.S.C. §552(b)(3), agencies may withhold particular records pursuant to other federal withholding statutes. The so-called b(3) exemption protects from disclosure any information that is specifically withheld from public release by a statute other than FOIA. For example, 18 U.S.C. §3509(d) provides authority for agencies to withhold certain

---

(...continued)
http://www.usdoj.gov/ag/foia-memo-march2009.pdf.

[61] Committee on Oversight and Government Reform, "Issa & Cummings Unveil FOIA Oversight and Implementation Act," press release, March 12, 2013, at http://oversight.house.gov/release/issa-cummings-unveil-foia-oversight-and-implementation-act/.

[62] Environmental Protect Agency, "About FOIAonline," at https://foiaonline regulations.gov/foia/action/public/home/about.

[63] The participating agencies are EPA, NARA, Department of Commerce, Department of the Treasury, the Federal Labor Relations Authority, and the Merit Systems Protection Board.

[64] Committee on Oversight and Government Reform, "Issa & Cummings Unveil FOIA Oversight and Implementation Act," press release, March 12, 2013, at http://oversight.house.gov/release/issa-cummings-unveil-foia-oversight-and-implementation-act/.

[65] OGIS was created in 2007 by the OPEN Government Act of 2007 (P.L. 110-175). OGIS is discussed in greater detail in the section entitled Oversight of the Office of Government Information Services in this report.

information that contains identifying information pertaining to children involved in criminal proceedings. Since the October 28, 2009, enactment of the OPEN FOIA Act of 2009 (P.L. 111-83), any prospective statute that exempts material from public release must also specifically cite FOIA to qualify for exemption. It had historically been difficult to keep track of existing and newly created b(3) FOIA exemptions or to systematically examine such exemptions prior to enactment of the 2009 requirement.

Since 2011, DOJ has provided online an annual list of all the b(3) exemptions that departments and agencies reported claiming in a fiscal year.[66] DOJ's "Summary of Annual FOIA Reports" and list of b(3) exemptions claimed for FY2012 show that federal agencies used 30,514 b(3) exemptions using 130 different b(3) statutes in FY2012—which is 5,579 (15.5%) fewer b(3) claims than in FY2011.[67] In FY2011, agencies cited 140 different b(3) statutes. In FY2012, therefore, agencies claimed fewer b(3) exemptions and cited fewer statutes to make those claims.

In some cases, however, an agency increased use of particular exemptions. According to DOJ's list of b(3) exemptions claimed by agencies, in FY2012 the DOD claimed 617 more exemptions than in FY2011 pursuant to 18 U.S.C. §798, which is related to "certain classified information pertaining to the communication, intelligence, and cryptographic devices of the United States or any foreign government."[68] Additionally in FY2012, the DOD claimed exemptions pursuant to 50 U.S.C. §403-1, which is related to "intelligence sources and methods".[69] In FY2012, DOD claimed the exemption 2,034 times. In FY2011, DOD claimed the exemption 561 times. It is not clear what statutory or policy changes may prompt increased use of this particular b(3) exemption. Agencies are not required to provide an explanation for increasing use of FOIA exemptions.

Oversight of the Office of Government Information Services

In addition to examining other substantive issues related to FOIA implementation, the 113th Congress may continue oversight of OGIS, an entity created in the OPEN Government Act of 2007.[70] OGIS is required by 5 U.S.C. §552 to

---

[66] See, for example, U.S. Department of Justice, "Statutes Used by Federal Departments and Agencies in Conjunction with Exemption 3 of the FOIA As Reported in Fiscal Year 2010 Annual FOIA Reports," at http://www.justice.gov/oip/docs/2010-exemption3-statutes.pdf.

[67] U.S. Department of Justice, "Summary of Annual FOIA Reports for FY2011," p. 8, at http://www.justice.gov/oip/foiapost/fy-2011-annual-report-summary.pdf; "Summary of Annual FOIA Reports for FY2012," p. 6 at http://www.justice.gov/oip/docs/fy2012-annual-report-summary.pdf; "Statutes Used by Federal Departments and Agencies in Conjunction with Exemption 3 of the FOIA As Reported in Fiscal Year 2011 Annual FOIA Reports," at http://www.justice.gov/oip/docs/2011-exemption3-statutes.pdf; "Statutes Used by Federal Departments and Agencies in Conjunction with Exemption 3 of the FOIA As Reported in Fiscal Year 2012 Annual FOIA Reports," at http://www.justice.gov/oip/docs/2012-exemption3-statutes.pdf.

[68] To determine the increase, CRS compared the claims between the FY2011 and the FY2012 b(3) exemption lists. See U.S. Department of Justice, "Statutes Used by Departments and Agencies in Conjunction with Exemption 3 of the FOIA as Reported in FY2012 Annual FOIA Reports," p. 3, at http://www.justice.gov/oip/docs/2012-exemption3-statutes.pdf; and "Statutes Used by Departments and Agencies in Conjunction with Exemption 3 of the FOIA as Reported in FY2011 Annual FOIA Reports," p. 3, at http://www.justice.gov/oip/docs/2011-exemption3-statutes.pdf.

[69] U.S. Department of Justice, "Statutes Used by Departments and Agencies in Conjunction with Exemption 3 of the FOIA as Reported in FY2011 Annual FOIA Reports," p. 6; and "Statutes Used by Departments and Agencies in Conjunction with Exemption 3 of the FOIA as Reported in FY2012 Annual FOIA Reports," p. 6.

[70] P.L. 110-175; 121 Stat. 2524.

- mediate disputes between FOIA requesters and federal agencies;
- review the policies and procedures of administrative agencies under FOIA;
- review agency compliance with FOIA; and
- recommend policy changes to the Congress and President to improve the administration of FOIA.[71]

As noted earlier in this report, DOJ is charged with ensuring that agencies comply with FOIA, and performs this mission by issuing guidance and conducting training.[72] DOJ also department defends federal agencies in FOIA-related litigation.[73] OGIS, in contrast, is charged with reviewing agencies' compliance with FOIA, recommending ways to improve FOIA administration, and mediating FOIA disputes that emerge between agencies and the public. OGIS has defined itself as a "FOIA ombudsman," seeking to facilitate "clear, direct communication" where it "has been lacking."[74]

Congress, at times, has encountered executive-branch resistance to FOIA amendments. OGIS's inception provides one such example. The OPEN Government Act of 2007[75] created OGIS to review FOIA policies and agency compliance as well as to recommend ways to improve FOIA. Pursuant to the OPEN Government Act, the office was to be placed within NARA. President George W. Bush's FY2009 budget recommendations, however, sought a repeal of the creation of OGIS and, instead, sought OGIS's enacted responsibilities be assigned to the Department of Justice.[76] In creating OGIS, legislators had purposefully placed it outside of the Department of Justice, which represents agencies sued by FOIA requesters.[77]

The 111th Congress responded to the Administration's recommendation by appropriating $1 million for OGIS and explicitly requiring its establishment within NARA.[78] OGIS began

---

[71] OGIS reviews agency policies and procedures, audits agency performance, recommends policy changes, and mediate disputes between FOIA requesters and agencies with a view to alleviating the need for litigation, while not limiting the ability of a requester to litigate FOIA claims.

[72] U.S. Department of Justice, "About the Office," at http://www.justice.gov/oip/about-us html.

[73] Ibid.

[74] U.S. Office of Government Information Services, "About OGIS," at https://ogis.archives.gov/about-ogis htm.

[75] P.L. 110-175; 121 Stat. 2524.

[76] U.S. Office of Management and Budget, *Budget of the United States Government, Fiscal Year 2009—Appendix* (Washington: GPO, 2008), p. 239. Sec. 519 of the budget recommendations read as follows:

> The Department of Justice shall carry out the responsibilities of the office established in 5 U.S.C. 552(h), from amounts made available in the Department of Justice appropriation for "General Administration Salaries and Expenses." In addition, subsection (h) of section 552 of title 5, United States Code, is hereby repealed, and subsections (i) through (l) are redesignated as (h) through (k).

[77] See Sen. Patrick Leahy, "Leahy: FOIA Ombudsman Belongs At Archives, Not DOJ," press release, February 14, 2008, http://www.leahy.senate.gov/press/leahy-foia-ombudsman-belongs-at-archives-not-doj; and Citizen Media Law Project, "Bush Refuses to Fund New FOIA Ombudsman, Takes the Heart Out of Open Government Reform Law," weblog, February 7, 2008, at http://www.citmedialaw.org/blog/2008/bush-refuses-fund-new-foia-ombudsman-takes-heart-out-open-government-reform-law.

[78] P.L. 111-8. See also U.S. Congress, House Committee on Appropriations, *Explanatory Statement to Accompany Omnibus Appropriations Act, 2009*, committee print, 111th Cong., 1st sess., p. 988, at http://www.gpo.gov/fdsys/pkg/CPRT-111JPRT47494/pdf/CPRT-111JPRT47494-DivisionD.pdf.

operations within NARA in September 2009.[79] Subsequent appropriations for OGIS have come from NARA's general appropriation and have not appeared as a separate line-item.

A Citizen's Guide to Using the Freedom of Information Act

The U.S. House of Representatives Committee on Government Reform published *A Citizen's Guide on Using the Freedom of Information Act and the Privacy Act of 1974 to Request Government Records*, most recently in September 2012.[80] In addition to the text of the acts, the *Citizen's Guide* contains descriptions and explanations of the FOIA administrative process, sample FOIA records request forms, and bibliographies of related congressional and noncongressional material. The *Citizen's Guide* is the only document that provides the public with details on how executive branch agencies should be administering FOIA, according to the congressional committee with jurisdiction over its administration.

Releasing Controversial Information

Congress has explicitly exempted certain controversial materials from public release under FOIA. For example, in the 111th Congress, the Department of Homeland Security Appropriations Act, 2010 (P.L. 111-83) exempted photographs of the treatment of certain individuals from public disclosure pursuant to FOIA.

Photographs That Could Potentially Endanger U.S. Citizens

Specifically, section 565 of P.L. 111-83 authorizes the Secretary of the Department of Defense to withhold from disclosure any photographic record that "would endanger citizens of the United States, members of the United States Armed Forces, or employees of the United States Government deployed outside the United States."[81] The law requires the photographs to have been taken between September 11, 2001, and January 22, 2009, and be "related to the treatment of individuals engaged, captured, or detained after September 11, 2001, by the Armed Forces of the United States in operations outside of the United States." Photographs are exempted from public release for three years, and it appears that the Secretary can extend that exemption in three year increments in perpetuity.[82]

Photographs and Video of Osama bin Laden

In April 2012, the United States District Court for the District of Columbia found in favor of the Central Intelligence Agency when it would not require that the agency release 52 records

---

[79] For more information on OGIS appropriations, see CRS Report R41340, *Financial Services and General Government (FSGG): FY2011 Appropriations*, coordinated by Garrett Hatch.

[80] U.S. Congress, House Committee on Government Reform, *A Citizen's Guide on Using the Freedom of Information Act and the Privacy Act of 1974 to Request Government Records*, H.Rept. 112-689, 112th Cong., 2nd sess. (Washington: GPO, 2012), at http://oversight.house.gov/wp-content/uploads/2012/09/Citizens-Guide-on-Using-FOIA.2012.pdf. The House Committee on Oversight and Government Reform (and its predecessor committees) has published ten editions of this report. The first edition of the guide was published in 1977.

[81] P.L. 111-83; 125 Stat. 2184-2185.

[82] Ibid.

responsive to Judicial Watch's FOIA request for "all photographs and/or video recordings of Osama (Usama) Bin Laden taken during and/or after the U.S. military operation in Pakistan on or about May 1, 2011."[83] In his memorandum opinion, Judge James E. Boasberg wrote:

> A picture may be worth a thousand words. And perhaps moving pictures bear an even higher value. Yet, in this case, verbal descriptions of the death and burial of Osama Bin Laden will have to suffice for this Court will not order the release of anything else.[84]

On October 16, 2012, Judicial Watch appealed the District Court's findings. On May 21, 2013, the District Court of Appeals affirmed the lower court's decision.

The Release of White House Visitor Logs

In September 2009, the White House agreed to release the Secret Service visitor sign-in logs maintained at the White House and the Vice Presidential Residence.[85] The logs track who enters either of the two locations.[86] The White House's decision to release the files followed three years of litigation with Citizens for Responsibility and Ethics in Washington (CREW), which filed the FOIA request with the Secret Service seeking access to sign-in logs.[87] Since December 2009, White House visitor records that are at least 90 to 120 days old have been publicly available.[88] Pursuant to the White House's policy, certain fields within the records may be redacted to protect "personal privacy or law enforcement concerns (e.g., dates of birth, social security numbers, and contact phone numbers); records that implicate the personal safety of [Executive Office of the President] staff (their daily arrival and departure); or records whose release would threaten national security interests."[89] Certain other records are also excepted from release, including "purely personal guests of the first and second families," "records related to a small group of particularly sensitive meetings (e.g., visits of potential Supreme Court nominees)," and "visitor information for the Vice President's Residence."[90] Visitor records created between January 20, 2009, and September 15, 2009, also are not included in the Secret Service visitor log release. Instead, the policy states that "the White House will respond voluntarily to individual requests submitted to the Counsel's Office that seek records during that time period, but only if the requests are reasonable, narrow, and specific."[91] The current practice of releasing the logs to the

---

[83] *Judicial Watch, Inc. v. Department of Defense*, 857 F. Supp. 2d 44 (D.D.C. 2012).

[84] Ibid., at 48.

[85] *Citizens for Responsibility and Ethics in Washington v. Department of Homeland Security*, 527 F. Supp. 2d 76 (D.D.C. 2007).

[86] The White House, "Visitor Records," at http://www.whitehouse.gov/briefing-room/disclosures/visitor-records.

[87] See *Citizens for Responsibility and Ethics in Washington v. Department of Homeland Security* 527 F. Supp. 2d 76 (D.D.C. 2007); *Citizens for Responsibility and Ethics in Washington v. Department of Homeland Security*, 527 F. Supp. 2d 76, 98 (D.D.C. 2007) (citing *Department of Justice v. Tax Analysts*, 492 U.S. at 147); *Citizens for Responsibility and Ethics in Washington v. Department of Homeland Security*, 532 F.3d 860 (D.C. Cir. 2008); and *Citizens for Responsibility and Ethics in Washington v. Department of Homeland Security*, No. 1:09-cv-01101 (D.D.C. 2009).

[88] The White House, "White House Voluntary Disclosure Policy Visitor Access Records," at http://www.whitehouse.gov/VoluntaryDisclosure.

[89] Ibid.

[90] Ibid. The policy does state it will release the number of people who visited the White House who would count toward the "small group of particularly sensitive meetings."

[91] Ibid.

public is the policy only of the current Administration, and would not necessarily carry over to future Administrations.

According to an April 2011 report by the Center for Public Integrity, the White House visitor logs "routinely omit or cloud key details about the identity of visitors, who they met with, the nature of the visit, and even includes the names of people who never showed up."[92]

On May 3, 2011, the House Energy and Commerce Committee's Subcommittee on Oversight and Investigations held a hearing entitled "White House Transparency, Visitor Logs, and Lobbyists." In his opening statement, Subcommittee Chairman Cliff Stearns said

> White House staff apparently purposely schedule meetings at the Caribou Coffee around the corner from the White House so that those meetings won't show up on the White House logs. And one executive branch agency even went so far as to require lobbyists to sign confidentiality agreements about their discussions with the administration.[93]

At the hearing, however, Anne Weisman, chief counsel from Citizens for Responsibility and Ethics in Washington, the organization that filed the lawsuit that prompted the White House to release the visitor logs, stated that she understood the limitations of the information provided by the Secret Service logs, noting that the logs were not meant to be used to determine who was meeting with the President and his staff. In her written testimony, Ms. Weisman stated the following:

> Some complain the visitor logs lack critical information, such as who the visitor is meeting with, and that requests for clearance were made by low-level staff in order to conceal the true nature of the visit. These criticisms reflect a fundamental misunderstanding of the nature of these logs and the purpose they serve. The White House visitor logs are not the equivalent of calendars or date books and, as every court to address this issue has found, are the records of the Secret Service, not the President. The Secret Service creates these records in furtherance of its statutory mission to protect the president, vice president, and their families, which necessarily extends to protecting the White House complex....
>
> To be clear, CREW disagrees with the legal position of the White House that these records are presidential and therefore not publicly accessible under the Freedom of Information Act. Nevertheless, we settled our litigation, which began under the Bush administration and continued under the Obama administration, over access to these records when the Obama White House offered to not only provide CREW with its requested records, but to post on the White House's website on an ongoing basis nearly all visitor records, subject to very limited and reasonable exceptions.[94]

---

[92] Fred Schulte and Viveca Novak, "White House visitor logs riddled with holes," *iWatchNews.com*, April 13, 2011, at http://www.iwatchnews.org/2011/04/13/4115/white-house-visitor-logs-riddled-holes.

[93] U.S. Congress, House Committee on Energy and Commerce, Subcommittee on Oversight and Investigations, *White House Transparency, Visitor Logs and Lobbyists*, 112th Cong., 1st sess., May 3, 2011, at http://www.gpo.gov/fdsys/pkg/CHRG-112hhrg70819/pdf/CHRG-112hhrg70819.pdf (p. 2). Additionally, one media report claimed White House staff were meeting with "lobbyists and political operatives" at a coffee shop near the White House to ensure the meetings were "not subject to disclosure on the visitors' log." See Eric Lichtblau, "Across From White House, Coffee With Lobbyists," *New York Times*, June 24, 2010, at http://www nytimes.com/2010/06/25/us/politics/25caribou.html.

[94] Ibid., at http://democrats.energycommerce.house.gov/sites/default/files/image_uploads/Testimony_05.03.11_Weismann.pdf.

Operations of *FOIAonline*

On October 1, 2012, the Environmental Protection Agency, the Department of Commerce, and NARA unveiled *FOIAonline*, an online portal that provides "the public one place to submit FOIA requests, track their progress, communicate with the processing agency, search other requests, access previously released responsive documents and file appeals with participating agencies."[95] According to a NARA press release, EPA created *FOIAonline* by retooling the capabilities of *Regulations.gov*, a federal web portal that "allows people to comment on Federal regulations and other agency regulatory actions."[96] *FOIAonline* cost the six participating agencies $1.3 million to launch, and is expected to avoid $200 million in FOIA administration costs for those agencies over five years.[97] Other executive branch agencies can also choose to join *FOIAonline*.

Sunshine in the Government, a coalition of media groups that advocate for more open government, wrote in an online blog posting that *FOIAonline* "promises to make it easier on agencies and requesters alike to keep track of requests and make the FOIA process more efficient."[98] Whether *FOIAonline* proves effective in the long run, however, remains to be seen.

Some Policy Options for the 113th Congress

Congress has the authority to use its oversight and legislative powers to modify FOIA and affect its implementation. Conversely, Congress may determine that FOIA operations and implementation are currently effective, and decide to take no action. This section of the report reviews ways in which Congress could amend FOIA or ensure that FOIA continues to be implemented in accordance with Congress's intentions.

Monitoring the Expansion of b(3) Exemptions

At hearings in March 2011, the House Committee on Oversight and Government Reform and the Senate Committee on the Judiciary discussed the growing number of FOIA b(3) exemptions.[99] At these hearings, several Members expressed interest in having a centralized collection of the existing universe of b(3) exemptions as well as having the opportunity to debate the merits and

---

[95] U.S. National Archives, "National Archives Joins Federal Agencies to Launch New Freedom of Information Act (FOIA) Online System," press release, October 1, 2012, at http://www.archives.gov/press/press-releases/2013/nr13-01.html. The participating agencies are EPA, NARA, Department of Commerce, Department of the Treasury, the Federal Labor Relations Authority, and the Merit Systems Protection Board. *FOIAonline* is not associated with *FOIA.gov*. The Department of Justice operates *FOIA.gov*, which allows users to examine the administrative data provided in executive branch agencies' annual FOIA reports. *FOIAonline*, in contrast, is the tool that six executive branch agencies employ to administer FOIA.

[96] Ibid. According to the press release, EPA "began looking at the feasibility of a FOIA portal in 2010."

[97] Ibid.

[98] Sunshine in the Government Coalition, "Sunshine in the Government Blog," October 1, 2012, at http://sunshineingov.wordpress.com/2012/10/01/feds-launch-new-tool-to-track-foia-requests-responses/.

[99] U.S. Congress, House Committee on Oversight and Government Reform, *The Freedom of Information Act: Crowd-Sourcing Government Oversight*, 112th Cong., 1st sess., March 17, 2011, H.Hrg. 112-19, (Washington: GPO, 2011); and U.S. Congress, Senate Committee on the Judiciary, *The Freedom of Information Act:Ensuring Transparency and Accountability in the Digital Age*, 112th Cong., 1st sess., March 15, 2011, S.Hrg. 112-296 (Washington: GPO, 2011).

scope of new b(3) exemption proposals. At the House hearing, Rick Blum, coordinator for the Sunshine in Government Initiative, suggested the committee

> take a hard look at these exemptions when they're proposed and make sure that they're absolutely necessary, that they're narrowly described, that they don't cover additional information, make sure that the drafting is narrow, make sure that they are publicly justified, and make sure that we have a chance to all weigh in.[100]

Giving committees with jurisdiction over FOIA implementation a chance to examine b(3) exemptions before their enactment may prevent the creation of exemptions written more broadly than intended. It also may prevent certain agencies from operating without the public being able to access data and records. Requiring each chamber to refer any legislation with a b(3) exemption to certain committees, however, might require rules changes in each chamber. Such requirements could slow down the legislative process, and, therefore, make it more difficult to enact protections for sensitive information or data.

Congress may also choose to require agencies that claim b(3) exemptions to publicly justify the need for that exemption. It is possible that every b(3) exemption is meritorious, but, in many cases, the public is not provided an opportunity to learn why the exemption was needed. Congress, for example, could require agencies, in their annual FOIA reports, to provide a policy justification, in plain language, for any b(3) exemption it claimed. To reduce time and resource burdens on agencies, Congress could narrow the scope of such reporting to justifications for the use of b(3) exemptions enacted in the past two years (the length of each Congress). Congress could also choose to amend FOIA to require that Congress include a policy justification that explains the need for any new withholding statute as a requirement for that statute to qualify as a b(3) exemption.

As noted in the "Use and Growth of Exemptions" section above, however, data demonstrate some agencies are increasing use of particular b(3) exemptions.[101] Requiring justifications for newly enacted b(3) statutes may promote greater public understanding for the creation of b(3) exemptions, but it may not help the public understand why an agency may increasingly rely on previously existing b(3) exemptions. Congress, therefore, may choose to require agencies to provide, in their annual reports, policy justifications for increasing use of b(3) exemptions. For example, Congress could require an agency to provide a policy justification for increasing use of a b(3) exemption if the agency's use of the exemption has met a particular numeric or percentage threshold when compared to the previous fiscal year.[102]

---

[100] U.S. Congress, House Committee on Oversight and Government Reform, *The Freedom of Information Act: Crowd-Sourcing Government Oversight*. The comment was made during the question and answer period and can be seen at http://www.youtube.com/watch?v=lNbMe8StyXw (4:40 mark).

[101] In some cases, agencies were claiming b(3) exemptions that it had previously not used. For example, in FY2012, the Department of Defense claimed 1,473 more exemptions than in FY2011 pursuant to 50 U.S.C. §403-1, which is related to "intelligence sources and methods." See U.S. Department of Justice, "Statutes Used by Departments and Agencies in Conjunction with Exemption 3 of the FOIA as Reported in FY2012 Annual Reports," p. 6 at http://www.justice.gov/oip/docs/2012-exemption3-statutes.pdf; and "Statutes Used by Departments and Agencies in Conjunction with Exemption 3 of the FOIA as Reported in FY2011 Annual FOIA Reports," p. 6, at http://www.justice.gov/oip/docs/2011-exemption3-statutes.pdf.

[102] In selecting a threshold amount, Congress may consider ways to minimize reporting requirements by selecting a threshold that captures only significant increases in the use of a b(3) exemption. Without such limitation, agencies could be required to provide a justification in any case when an agency increased use of a b(3) exemption by only one or two claims.

Consideration of Agencies' FOIA Culture

Congress may be interested in ensuring that all agencies are implementing the most effective FOIA practices and creating a more transparent operating culture. Among the ways to examine FOIA culture are by reviewing DOJ's chief FOIA officers summary report, assessing improvements in agencies' FOIA customer service, and requiring agencies to ensure their FOIA regulations are up-to-date.

The Department of Justice's Chief FOIA Officer Reports

The Office of Information Policy (OIP) within the Department of Justice, in compliance with federal law (5 U.S.C. §552(e)(1)), annually compiles a summary of all agency Chief FOIA Officer reports and offers recommendations to improve FOIA compliance. These reports include information on outstanding FOIA requests, FOIA backlog reduction efforts, b(3) exemptions claimed to deny requests, and actions that agencies take to make certain its employees are aware of new or modified transparency policies. According to the annual reports, agencies have taken a variety of steps to influence their internal FOIA culture, including attending FOIA training—with some training occurring online, assessing for adequate staffing levels, and making record disclosures prior to the filing of a FOIA request for such records (often called proactive disclosures).[103] Other agencies have voluntarily used *Facebook*, *Twitter*, and *YouTube* to webcast meetings or publicize recent information and records releases.

In OIP's 2013 summary report, which is the most current one available, the office offered three guidelines in which the office determined agencies could further improve their administration of FOIA:

1. Focus on quality training—specifically, the guidance recommends that agencies make FOIA training available to their employees at least once per year.
2. Focus on processing simpler requests within 20 or fewer days.
3. Focus on closing their 10 oldest requests.[104]

Congress may require agencies to adopt some, none, or all of OIP's recommendations. Congress may require agencies to change FOIA processing policies that are not addressed in OIP's recommendations, including requiring the use of social media to notify the public of the release of records or of their withholding.

---

[103] U.S. Department of Justice, Office of Information Policy, "Summary of Agency Chief FOIA Officer Reports for 2012 and Assessment of Agency Progress in Implementing the President's FOIA Memorandum and the Attorney General's FOIA Guidelines With OIP Guidance for Further Improvement," August 2012, at http://www.justice.gov/oip/docs/sum-2012-chief-foia-officer-rpt.pdf.

[104] U.S. Department of Justice, Office of Information Policy, Summary of Agency Chief FOIA Officer Reports for 2013 and Assessment of Agency Progress in Implementing the President's FOIA Memorandum and the Attorney General's FOIA Guidelines With OIP Guidance for Further Improvement, Washington, DC, pp. 24-25, at http://www.justice.gov/oip/docs/2013-cfo-assessment.pdf.

Improving Customer Service

Past OIP guidance has recommended improvements in customer service.[105] The FY2012 summary report does not explicitly address customer service. OGIS, however, in its guidance to agencies on how to best avoid FOIA-related litigation, stated that some agencies do not speak to requesters "regarding their requests—at all."[106] The OGIS guidance continued:

> We have observed that communication with requesters is not only good customer service, but it the single most efficient and cost-effective way to avoid disputes. Requesters have told us that if an agency at least lets them know what is going on with their request, they will be less likely to file suit in those cases.[107]

Congress may choose to oversee whether those who make FOIA requests are receiving appropriate and clear responses from employees who administer FOIA.

Updating Agencies' FOIA Regulations

In December 2012, the National Security Archive[108] released a report that found 62 of 99 federal agencies that administer FOIA requests have not updated their FOIA regulations since Attorney General Eric Holder's March 2009 memorandum on FOIA.[109] The report found that 56 agencies had not updated their FOIA regulations since enactment of the OPEN Government Act of 2007 (P.L. 110-175; 121 Stat. 2524); 12 agencies had not updated their regulations since enactment of the Electronic FOIA Amendments of 1996 (P.L. 104-231; 110 Stat. 3048).[110] These amendments included provisions that

- determine how agencies may assess and impose fees on FOIA requesters for the costs associated with responding to their FOIA requests;
- clarified the time agencies have to comply with a request; and
- required the creation of a tracking system that allows requesters to know the status of their requests.

Agencies that have not updated their regulations, therefore, may be administering the FOIA contrary to the law, as amended.

---

[105] U.S. Department. of Justice, Office of Information Policy, "FOIA Post: Summary of Agency Chief FOIA Officer Reports with Finding and OIP Guidance for Improvement," July 29, 2010, at http://www.justice.gov/oip/foiapost/2010foiapost23.htm.

[106] U.S. Office of Government Information Services, "How to Invite a FOIA Lawsuit," at http://blogs.archives.gov/foiablog/2012/02/03/how-to-invite-a-foia-lawsuit/.

[107] Ibid.

[108] The National Security Archive is a collection of journalists and scholars that seeks to defend and expand "public access to information." See The National Security Archive, "About the National Security Archive" at http://www.gwu.edu/~nsarchiv/nsa/the_archive.html. The study is available at The National Security Archive, "Outdated Agency Regs Undermine the Freedom of Information," at http://www.gwu.edu/~nsarchiv/NSAEBB/NSAEBB405/.

[109] U.S. Department of Justice, Attorney General Eric Holder, *Memorandum For the Heads of Executive Departments and Agencies: The Freedom of Information Act (FOIA)*, Washington, DC, March 19, 2009, pp. 1-2 at http://www.usdoj.gov/ag/foia-memo-march2009.pdf.

[110] The National Security Archive," Outdated Agency Regs Undermine Freedom of Information," December 4, 2012, at http://www.gwu.edu/~nsarchiv/NSAEBB/NSAEBB405/.

Congress, therefore, may wish to consider whether it should direct agencies to examine their FOIA regulations, to determine whether they reflect statutory amendments, and to update any regulations that do not reflect FOIA, as amended.

Status of White House Visitor Logs

The 113th Congress may consider enacting legislation that would determine whether Secret Service logs that contain information on visitors to the White House should be made publicly available or should remain protected records.[111] For example, Congress may create legislation that explicitly states whether the White House visitor logs should be treated as "presidential records" pursuant to the Presidential Records Act. If so, the records would be afforded additional protections that could delay their release by up to 20 years.[112] If the logs were determined not to be "presidential records," they would be subject to public release unless a FOIA exemption applied. Codifying treatment of the logs would require the Secret Service to release the logs regardless of who occupies the White House. As noted earlier in this report, the current practice of releasing the records is the policy only of the current Administration, and would not necessarily carry over to future Administrations. Other legislative options might include (1) amending FOIA to create a specific exemption for the Secret Service logs, which would allow the Secret Service to withhold them from public release; (2) modifying the laws that govern operations of the Secret Service, clarifying whether Secret Service records are governed by FOIA, the Presidential Records Act, or by some other records policies; or (3) determining whether any legislation should be applied retroactively to the records of the previous presidential administrations, or if the policy should apply only to current and future Secret Service logs. Congress may opt to take no action, thereby permitting the continued voluntary and limited release of such records under the Obama Administration.

Examining the Progress of *FOIAonline*

Congress may choose to continue oversight of the progress of *FOIAonline*, the new FOIA administration tool developed by the Environmental Protection Agency.[113] As of August 2013, six agencies are employing *FOIAonline* in their implementation of FOIA.[114] Congress could direct the Government Accountability Office (GAO) or an agency inspector general to audit *FOIAonline* to see if it is allowing agencies to appropriately administer FOIA and reduce the costs to administer it. If an audit finds that the tool is successful, Congress may choose to require other agencies or components of agencies to adopt the *FOIAonline* technology. If the study shows that

---

[111] If Congress opted to create such legislation, it could do so by amending FOIA (5 U.S.C. §552), Presidential Records Act (44 U.S.C. §2201), or the Secret Service Statute (18 U.S.C. §3056) to explicitly state the status of the Secret Service logs. For more information on presidential records, see CRS Report R40238, *The Presidential Records Act: Background and Recent Issues for Congress*, by Wendy Ginsberg.

[112] Pursuant to the Presidential Records Act, an outgoing President can restrict access to certain records for up to 12 years (44 U.S.C. §2204(a)). After 12 years, the President's records are then subject to release pursuant to FOIA's provisions. The 20-year protection assumes a record was created in January of a 2-term (8-year) President's first term. The 12-year restriction to record access begins at the end of a President's tenure. For more information on the PRA, see CRS Report R40238, *The Presidential Records Act: Background and Recent Issues for Congress*, by Wendy Ginsberg.

[113] See "Operations of *FOIAonline*" above. *FOIAonline* is found at https://foiaonline.regulations.gov/foia/action/public/home.

[114] The participating agencies are EPA, NARA, Department of Commerce, Department of the Treasury, the Federal Labor Relations Authority, and the Merit Systems Protection Board.

FOIAonline is not appropriately administering FOIA, or that it has experienced unintended additional costs, Congress may choose to prevent agencies from adopting the technology.

An Alternative for FOIA Implementation: Centralizing FOIA Processing

Congress also may choose to address the uneven implementation of FOIA across executive branch departments and agencies. As noted earlier in this report, some agencies appear to have dramatically reduced their FOIA backlogs and have taken steps to modify their culture to enhance the processing of FOIA requests, while other agencies appear to have been less aggressive in making changes to their FOIA implementation. Congress may continue using its oversight powers in an effort to ensure that each agency is implementing FOIA according to congressional intent. Conversely, Congress could relocate FOIA request processing outside of individual agencies and create a new federal entity that would focus exclusively on answering FOIA requests. Congress may also require an existing agency to process all FOIA requests. Employees within the "FOIA processing agency" could determine which federal departments or agencies possesses requested records, and then apply FOIA to determine whether requested records would be released.

Creating a new entity to implement FOIA would likely have costs and benefits. For example, a single FOIA processing entity may be able to apply FOIA more consistently across the federal government than the dispersion of FOIA offices currently stationed within each federal department and agency. A centralized FOIA entity, however, may not understand the sensitivity of certain documents held within individual agencies. Departments and agencies would likely be reluctant to relinquish control over the dissemination of their records. Centralizing FOIA implementation may initially increase costs through the hiring and training of staff and securing of office space. The centralized office, however, may decrease long-term costs by eliminating the need for certain FOIA positions that currently are replicated in each federal agency—including multiple FOIA attorneys, administrative assistants, and archival researchers.

If Congress were to create a centralized FOIA agency, there are a number of places it could be housed. For example, Congress might place the agency within the Department of Justice, which currently defends agencies if lawsuits result from FOIA implementation. Congress might place the processing entity within NARA, which houses OGIS—also known as the FOIA ombudsman. Congress also might establish a "FOIA processing agency" as an independent entity that reports directly to the President and Congress. Congress could elect to give the agency greater independence from the President, as it did with the Social Security Administration and the Office of Special Counsel.[115]

---

[115] Mechanisms that establish greater independence include, for example, protection from arbitrary removal by the President. See 5 U.S.C. §1211 and 42 U.S.C. §902.

Author Contact Information

Wendy Ginsberg
Analyst in American National Government
wginsberg@crs.loc.gov, 7-3933

Acknowledgments

Andrea DeWald, Research Associate, contributed to this report.

www.ingramcontent.com/pod-product-compliance
Lightning Source LLC
Chambersburg PA
CBHW081818170526

45167CB00008B/3456

9781503008861